1st edition

How to Change Your Name in Texas

By Attorney Richard S. Granat

FIRST EDITION   SEPTEMBER 2014

Editor   Pamela Andrews

Technology   Gregor Weeks

Cover Design   GRANATDESIGN, LLC.

Proofreader   Nancy Wruble

Printing   Amazon

SmartLegalForms is an imprint of SmartLegalForms®, Inc.
SmartLegalForms is a trademark of SmartLegalForms®, Inc.
Manufactured in the United States of America

Granat, Richard

How to Change Your Name in Texas / by Richard S. Granat -1st ed.

Registration Code: NAMTEXADULT20142054

UPDATE SERVICE AND FILLABLE FORMS

All legal content in this product was up-to-date during publication. If you register your product using the Registration Code on this page and your email address at http://www.texasnamechangelaw.com you will receive any legal form updates since this book was published and you can download the legal forms in Adobe .PDF fillable format for no additional charge. This is a free service.

If you purchase this book online and we have your email address your product is registered automatically and you will be sent a free copy of the Adobe .PDF fillable forms automatically.

Please note this self-help legal formbook is not a substitute for personalized legal advice from a lawyer who practices in the jurisdiction where you live. We do not provide legal advice.

Table of Contents

Introduction to Name Change for an Adult in Texas

n Texas, an adult who wishes to change his or her name must be a resident of Texas for at least six months, must file a Petition in the District Court of the county where he or she resides, and must be a resident of the County for at least ninety days as detailed below. The Petition informs the Court of the Petitioner's name, the name the Petitioner wishes to assume, the reasons for the change and other personal information required by statute. The Petition must be notarized.

A party filing a Petition for Name Change for an adult presents to the District Court a set of fingerprints of the person whose name is to be changed. The Petitioner is responsible for the costs of obtaining fingerprints and other costs which may be incurred upon filing.

Once you file your Petition for Name Change, schedule a time to ask the Judge to approve your name change. The Court conducts a hearing and then renders final judgment by entering an Order of approval of name change.

Granting a Petition for change of name is discretionary with the Court, and the Court may deny a Petition on grounds. For an Order of name change to be granted, the Court must find sufficient reasons for the change and also find the name change in the interest or to the benefit of the Petitioner and in the interest of the public. A person may not change their name to avoid judgments or legal actions against him or her, or to avoid debts and obligations. A person cannot change their name to defraud another person.

The law which governs name changes in Texas is Texas Family Code, chapter 45. The Courts are often willing to accept name changes for almost any legitimate reason. However, granting a Petition for Change of Name is discretionary with the Court. For an order of name change to be granted, the Court must find compliance with the requirements of notice and the requirements for the allegations in the Petition. The Court must also find good and sufficient reason for the change and find the change consistent with the public interest.

County Variations

Except where specifically noted, we have attempted to include every document that you will need to file for the name change. These documents and instructions have been designed to meet the requirements set by Texas. It is possible that county variations exist in the documents and/or filing instructions. Some variation in terminology may also exist (some counties may use a Petition, while others may use a Complaint, even though they are the same document). We are not able to plan for every possible county variation. Please understand that adjustments may need to be made to meet variations to local documents and/or procedures. Please work with your court clerk to ensure that adjustments are accurate

Eligibility for Changing Your Name in Texas

Requirements to File for a Change of Name for an Adult in Texas

Texas law requires certain things before you can file for a name change (for an adult) and/or during the name change process in Texas. These requirements include:

- You must have lived in Texas for the last 6 months.
- You must have lived in your county for the last 90 days.
- You must not have been convicted of any crime, felony and/or misdemeanor.
- You must not be currently under indictment for a crime, felony and/or misdemeanor.
- You must not be requesting the name change to avoid creditors.
- You must not be involved in a bankruptcy proceeding.
- You must be an adult, 18 years of age or older.
- You must attach a complete set of your fingerprints to your petition at time of filing.

Transgendered Name Changes

Some courts in Texas may prefer that a party wishing to file for a name change due to transgender surgery wait until such time as the surgery has been completed. The local Court Clerk in the County in which you will be filing will have more specific information on the local Court's preference and requirements.

Exceptions for the Use of this Product

If you are only correcting a first or middle name AND you were born in Texas, you may NOT need to go through the court-ordered process. We recommend that you contact the Vital Records Department/Agency in Texas. Contact information for the Texas State Vital Records Office can be found at http://www.vitalrec.com/tx.html. You may also want to contact your local Court Clerk for further information.

Name Change and Bankruptcy

These name change forms are for simple uncontested name change actions only. Attempting to change one's name when contemplating filing for bankruptcy and/or after one has claimed bankruptcy can be complicated and our name change pleadings are not applicable in such situations. These situations would typically require the assistance of an attorney who is a member of the bar in the state in which you live.

Changing Your Name after Marriage or Divorce

Name changes subsequent to marriage or divorce are common in this day and age. A person may want to adopt the surname of her spouse upon marriage or may want to return to using her former name with a divorce. The process for changing a name after a marriage or divorce is relatively simple and does not typically involve the lengthy process required for name changes.

Frequently Asked Questions about Name Change

Changing Your Name

Any person may change his name if the change is not for a fraudulent purpose. Reasons for a name change are varied and personal. The person may dislike his given name, want his name to reflect his heritage or religious views, want to disassociate himself from a former lifestyle, or may need to change it for security and protection purposes.

Laws require courts to grant an application for a name change unless a prohibition does not allow the change. For instance, a person convicted of a felony cannot change his name since law enforcement has a substantial interest in tracking his location.

While all states have statutes setting forth procedures for legally changing your name, the procedures vary from state to state.

Most states require a court order to legalize a name change, so contact your local Clerk of Court to find out whether your particular state allows name change by common usage.

What do I have to do to change my name?

If your state allows name change by common usage, you may use your new name. If your state requires a court order to effectuate a name change, you will need to file the papers and pay the filing fees before an order changing your name is issued. The Court, however, has the discretion to deny your request if it finds an unreasonable motive. The following reasons are likely to be good reasons by the Court: to shorten your name, to distance yourself from your family, or to use your stage name. You will also need to publish your name change in a local paper.

TIP

Remember although your state might allow name change by common usage, obtaining a court order may save you a lot of trouble in the long run. Your new name will be easier to prove and is more likely to be accepted if you have a court order to back it up. Your bank may be reluctant to change your name on your bank account if you have no court order evidencing the name change.

What are some of the most popular reasons for a person changing his/her name?

Name changes are sought for many reasons. Perhaps you simply do not like your birth name and want a name that better suits you. Perhaps you're divorced and did not request that the Court restore your maiden name as part of the divorce proceedings and your state does not offer a simplified procedure, such as California. Perhaps you are making or have made a career change, and feel that your birth name hinders you in your new job. As far as the reason(s) for your change of name, the reason(s) should be valid enough that a Judge would at least accept it/them. Remember that the reason(s) will go a long way in helping the Judge determine whether or not to grant your petition.

Name changes are common and are typically pretty easy to carry out. Our self-help name change forms contain detailed filing instructions to help you successfully change your name without the cost of an attorney.

Can I pick any name I want?

Yes, but there are a few limitations:
- The name cannot be chosen with fraudulent intent. You can avoid no judgments against you by changing your name.
- You cannot choose a name intentionally confusing, such as one with numbers or symbols. This means no person cannot refer to herself as "&" (ampersand); however, the symbol will never be his legal name, e.g., it will not ever appear on a passport.
- Your name cannot be a racial slur, nor can it contain threatening or obscure words, or words likely to incite violence. Names that are obscene or vulgar cannot be legally obtained. A person may use such a name, but he cannot have his name legally changed.
- Your name cannot interfere with any trademarked name or with the rights of another (e.g., the name of a famous person employed in a similar field).

What are the fees involved with a name change application?

Charges you may incur in the filing of any legal pleading with a court could include: filing fees, postage for certified mailings, fees associated with the signatures and seals of a Notary Public, publication fees and service of process charges. It is difficult to determine exactly what fees will be needed due to the varying circumstances surrounding any legal action or case. Moreover, the processes and requirements for a name change application vary sometimes from county to county or even courthouse to courthouse. We recommend that you contact your local Court Clerk for information regarding the exact current cost of these fees.

How long will the entire application for change of name take?

Name change actions can take anywhere from a day to six months (sometimes even longer). The time it takes for such action to be ordered/decreed varies not only from county to county, but sometimes from courthouse to courthouse as well. Should time be a major factor for you, to see how long a name change at your local courthouse will take to process, we recommend that you contact the courthouse where you anticipate filing your particular legal action.

Can the entire procedure take place online or will a court appearance be necessary?

You should file your forms in-person at your local courthouse. This is the fastest, easiest and best approach to filing. Besides appearing to file your documents/forms, name change actions often require other appearances within court.

If you have further questions regarding court appearances pertaining to a name change application, we recommend that you contact your local Court Clerk with your questions.

If I was born in Florida but have since moved to Texas, in which state should I file my application for change of name?

In order to file for a name change, one must meet the residency requirements of the state in which he/she wishes to file. In other words, in order to petition a state for name change, you must be a permanent resident of that state. All states require a Petitioner/Applicant to be a resident of the state -- often for at least six months and sometimes for as long as one year -- before filing for a name change there. To file in Texas, you must have lived in the state for at least six months, and in the county of filing for at least ninety days, prior to filing. Someone who files for a name change, typically, must offer proof that (s)he has resided there for the required length of time.

I am only interested in changing my first name. Do your forms apply to this circumstance?

Our name change forms are applicable to changes of the first name, middle name, last name and/or any combination.

I am getting married. Will I have to do anything special to use my spouse's name?

A woman need not do anything to use her spouse's name; a certified copy of the marriage certificate is all the proof needed (but remember that you still must take the steps discussed above to notify others of your new name). A man, however, may need to obtain a court order to use his spouse's name.

I recently got married. Can I add my wife's last name to mine?

Yes. When a couple marries, they have several options when choosing which surname to use (traditionally, the wife takes her husband's last name). One of these options is hyphenation of both names by both spouses, and it is valid and acceptable.

I am getting divorced. Can I have my old name back?

Yes. The judge enters an order in the divorce decree restoring your former name. If the order is entered, a certified copy of the divorce decree will be sufficient documentation of the name change. You can have your maiden name restored as part of the divorce process.

Are your name change forms appropriate in adoption proceedings or paternity actions?

Our name change products and services are not to be used in connection with an adoption or paternity action, since in such cases the name change should be done as part of that case or proceeding.

What if someone files an objection to my request?

In the event that anyone files an objection to your request, your case will become a contested case and you are strongly urged to hire an attorney. If you do not retain an attorney you will have to represent yourself in a contested hearing.

What if the request to change my name is denied?

Most name change Petitions are granted, however, the law gives the Court the power to decline a person's request for a name change. Therefore, the Court can refuse a name change request if there is a reason to decline the request.

If a name change Petition was denied because there was not enough evidence to support the request, then you will have to wait until the circumstances that led to the denial change before you can file another Petition. This is because once the Court makes a decision about an incident or an event; it cannot address that same incident or event again. If the Petition was denied because of a procedural error (for example, you did not file the correct forms), then you should correct the error and request another time to ask the Judge to approve your name change.

Finally, whenever you lose in Court, you have the right to request the Court to reconsider its decision and you have the right to appeal the decision to a higher Court. Please note that in most cases you have 30 days or less from the date of the Judge's decision to exercise these rights or you may lose your right to reconsideration or appeal. You should seek the assistance of an attorney to exercise these rights.

What do I have to do after I get my new name?

The first step is to obtain a new driver's license and Social Security card with your new name. This will to facilitate changing your name with other agencies and institutions. You can start by applying at your local Social Security office. You will need to bring proof of your former name, such as your driver's license, and a certified copy of the Court's Order changing your name. To obtain a new driver's license, you must present a certified copy of the Court Order to the Department of Motor Vehicle office in your state.

Then, you need to contact any business or government agencies with which you deal to notify them of your new name and request it be changed in their records. Some important agencies to notify are your employer, school, creditors, utility companies, banks and financial institutions, insurance and mortgage companies, post office, Internal Revenue Service, registrar of voters, professional associations and frequent flier programs.

You also need to notify the passport office and Bureau of Records or Vital Statistics (to obtain a birth certificate with your new name). Be sure to change your name on any legal papers, such as wills, trusts, or contracts. More information on this topic may be found below.

Can I obtain a birth certificate with my new name?

Yes. However, the laws in your state may only permit issuance of an amended birth certificate rather than a new original birth certificate.

Is it possible to have a new passport issued reflecting my name change?

Yes. You must apply for an amended passport by completing a Passport Amendment/Validation Application (Form DS-19). You will have to provide a certified copy of the court order and your old passport.

I changed my name last year but do not like it as much as I thought I would. Can I change it back?

Probably, but follow the same procedure required for you to change it. Remember that discretion to allow a name change rests with the Court, and the Court will not look favorably on frequent name changes. Select a name you like and will be comfortable using.

Forms and Detailed Filing Instructions

Getting Started

All of your documents will eventually be filed in the District Court in the jurisdiction in which you reside. You must have lived within the State of Texas for six months and the County in which you will be filing your application in for at least ninety days.

You should contact the District Court you will be filing your Name Change action with by telephone PRIOR to filing to determine how you can obtain the required fingerprint cards (Texas Department of Public Safety or Federal Bureau of Investigation). You should be able to locate the phone number of the District Court(s) located in your county by referring to the Government Listings (the "blue pages") contained in your local phone book or on the Internet.

Many counties, such as Travis County, have the fingerprint cards available on-site. In such cases, you will need to pick up the fingerprint cards from your local courthouse. If your local courthouse does not have the fingerprint cards, ask the Clerk of said courthouse where you can obtain the fingerprint cards. Follow the directions of the Clerk to obtain the cards. As mentioned above, you must attach to the Petition (as Exhibit 'A"), upon filing, a legible and complete set of your fingerprints.

Here is some other information you may want to obtain from the Clerk's office:

1. Obtain the mailing address of the Court and the street address if it differs from the mailing address. Also, obtain driving directions if need be.

2. Ask the cost of the required filing fee. The fee sometimes differs from county to county.

3. Ask if you need to file documents specific to your local Court along with the standard Texas documents we have included. If there are additional documents, find out how you can obtain them.

4. Ask if there are any other special filing requirements that you should be aware of. Some counties, such as Travis County and Montgomery County, require that all civil cases filed in the District Court Clerk's office shall have attached a Civil Case Information Sheet that will be prepared by the District Court Clerk. Additionally, they require that all pleadings, motions, orders and other papers, including exhibits attached thereto, when offered for filing or entry, shall be descriptively titled and punched at the top of the page to accommodate Clerk's 2.75" center-to-center flat-filing system. By calling your local District Court in advance, you will be aware of such requirements upon filing.

5. Ask how many copies of each document or form are required. The majority of Courts only require the original – some may require an additional copy or two. (NOTE: Even if only the original is required, it is always a good idea to have extra copies on-hand.)

The Forms

There are three basic forms:

1. Original Petition for Change of Name of Adult

2. Order Granting Change of Name of Adult

3. Texas Civil Case Information Sheet

Since the documents are straightforward and self-explanatory, we have not provided line-by-line instructions for completing each item of the forms. However, we have included the following instructions to help you complete certain sections of the forms:

    1. **Cause No.:** The Clerk of the Court will complete this section when you file your papers. Since you don't have a Cause Number yet these spaces should remain blank for now. However, if at some point in the future you must file additional documents as part of this same name change action, you should insert the number(s) assigned by the Court.

    2. **Judicial District:** Again, the Clerk of the Court will complete this section when you file your papers. Since you don't have a Judicial District yet these spaces should remain blank for now. However, if at some point in the future you must file additional documents as part of this same name change action, you should insert the number(s) assigned by the Court.

    3. **Reason for Change of Name:** As far as the reasons for your change of name, you should simply put the reason that you want to change your name. This should be a valid enough reason that a Judge would at least accept it.

    4. **Street Address:** Enter your street address and include any unit or apartment number if applicable. A physical address must be provided. A "P.O. Box" or other mailing address cannot be used.

    5. **County:** Enter the name of your county of residence. Do not add the word "County" after the name.

    6. **City of Birth:** Enter the city where you were born.

    7. **Driver's License:** Designate the license number and state of issue for each driver's license you have possessed in the past 10 years (one entry at a time). Enter your current driver's license number first, then list any past licenses in chronological order from newest to oldest.

    8. **Texas Civil Case Information Sheet**: The included Civil Case Information Sheet is only a sample document. The Civil Case Information Sheet usually varies from county to county. Thus, if your court will not accept our general document, you should

obtain your court's local variation of the Civil Case Information Sheet upon your first filing and complete this document in black ink.

Additionally, all date spaces for certifying, filing, etc., should be left blank. Such spaces have to be filled-in later (in black ink) when certifying (notarizing), filing, etc. The Clerk may even date-stamp your documents when you file. In light of such, we always recommend that all dates like this be left blank - since they have to be filled-in on the date the document is filed, certified by a notary, etc.

You MUST label your fingerprint cards as Exhibit 'A' and attach them to the Petition accordingly.

The Petition should NOT be signed outside of the presence of a Notary Public. Your signature must be witnessed and notarized by the Notary. (Most courts and banks have a Notary Public on staff that will be able to help you. The fee is usually not more than a few dollars or less per document.) NOTE: Do not make any copies of the documents until the documents are notarized. Upon signing the Petition, in front of the Notary, your Petition now becomes a Verified Petition.

Important Note! Make sure to get your documents notarized. Failure to do so is the most common reason for being denied a change of name.

Make copies of each of the documents. You will keep the copies for your records and bring them to court with you upon each appearance or filing. We recommend making at least three copies of each of these documents. Again, do not make copies of documents until they are notarized.

Initial Filing

File the Petition and Civil Case Information Sheet, if applicable, (these documents should be hand delivered to the Court Clerk) in the District Court in the jurisdiction in which you reside and pay the filing fee. Filing fees may differ from county to county. Typically, only cash, money orders, or personal in-state checks will be accepted. You should contact your local Court to determine the exact filing fee, methods of payment accepted as well as to whom the check should be made payable.

This first filing should include:

1. The Original Petition and copies of this document.

2. Texas Civil Case Information Sheet.

3. Filing fee – typically should be a check or money order.

The Clerk will file your original documents and should stamp your copy(ies) and then give them back to you. These stamped copies are hereafter referred to as "file-stamped" copies.

At this time, as indicated above, the Clerk will assign your case a "Cause Number" and a "Judicial District". Make note of these assignments (your Cause Number and your Judicial District) because in the future when you file your signed Order document as part of this same name change action, you will need to insert the Cause Number and Judicial District assigned by the Court in your document.

Once you file your Petition and Civil Case Information Sheet, if applicable, ask the Clerk how to schedule a meeting with a Judge for your name change documents to be reviewed by the Court.

Day of Your Hearing

On the day of your hearing, make sure that you arrive at the courthouse at least thirty minutes early. Get your file from the District Court Clerk's office. Remember: At this point, you Order should be filled out except for the Judge's signature. Typically, upon checking in, the Clerk/bailiff will direct you to the appropriate courtroom.

You should take with you all paperwork that has not yet been submitted and copies of what has already been submitted. You should expect that the hearing will be informal, may or may not be recorded by a Court reporter, and, as long as there are no objections (see below), it may not last more than ten minutes.

Answer the Judge's questions with respect for the Court. Do not interrupt the Judge or volunteer information and always call the Judge "Your Honor." You should expect the Judge's line of questioning to be somewhat similar to the following:

Do you truthfully swear that the statements in the Petition are true and accurate?

What is your name and address?

How long have you been a resident of Texas and [County]?

What is the new name you are seeking?

Is the name change being done for a fraudulent purpose?

What is the reason for wanting to change your name?

If the Court is satisfied that the required information has been provided in the Petition, that the change of name is in the interest or to the benefit of the Petitioner and in the public interest, and if there are no reasonable objections to the name change, the Court may grant the Order (complete and sign the Order Granting Change of Name of Adult) authorizing your change of name.

File the signed Order and return your file at the District Court Clerk's office.

Request your Change of Name Certificate (from the Court).

The District Court Clerk's office will stamp the Order signed by the Judge. Once the Order is signed, your name is legally changed. After the name change has been finalized, you should request certified copies of the Order document. Usually, the first certified copy is free (included in the filing fee charge). Additional certified copies will cost a nominal fee and must be paid separately. Therefore, you should plan on having additional money available for the certified copies.

Objections to Your Request

In the event that anyone files an objection to your request, your case will become a contested case and you are strongly urged to hire an attorney. If you do not retain an attorney you will have to represent yourself in a contested hearing.

Implementing Your Change of Name

After your change of name has been finalized (ordered/decreed) you should notify several agencies.

• The Social Security Administration - fill out the "Request for Change in Social Security Records" form at your local Social Security Office. You will need a form of identification with your old name and a certified copy of the signed Order. More information is available at 1-800-772-1213 or online at http://ssa-custhelp.ssa.gov/app/answers/detail/a_id/315/;

• Motor Vehicle Administration (driver's license and car registration) - take a certified copy of the Court Order to the State Department of Motor Vehicles (Department of Public Safety – www.txdps.state.tx.us);

• Voter Registration - take a certified copy of the Court Order to the main Board of Elections office;

• Birth Certificates – Bureau of Vital Statistics. (888-963-7111 and/or http://www.dshs.state.tx.us/VS/);

• State Income Tax - send a letter (including the old name and Social Security Number) and a certified copy of the Court Order to the State Department of Taxation (there is no need to send anything for Federal Taxes since the Social Security Administration will contact the Internal Revenue Service directly);

• Recorded Deeds, Passports, Welfare Payments, Alimony Payments, Selective Service, the United States Postal Service, Passport Office, etc.

• You may also wish to contact other places as well such as your bank. Should you need extra copies of the Order they should be available from the Clerk's office at a nominal fee.

Additionally, after changing one's name, it is always a good idea to revise any legal documents that are in force that may include your name.

CAUSE NO._____

IN THE MATTER OF THE:	§	IN THE DISTRICT COURT OF
	§	
	§	
	§	
	§	
CHANGE OF NAME OF	§	_____ COUNTY, TEXAS
_____	§	
	§	
	§	
	§	
	§	JUDICIAL DISTRICT _____
AN ADULT	§	
	§	
	§	

ORIGINAL PETITION FOR CHANGE OF NAME OF ADULT

TO THE HONORABLE JUDGE OF THIS COURT:

This suit is brought by _____, Petitioner, who resides at _____, _____ County, Texas. Petitioner is an adult.

In support of this request and in accordance with Section 45.102 of the Texas Family Code, I provide the following information about myself:

1. No discovery is intended.

2. My current full name is

_____.

3. My date of birth is

_____.

4. I was born in

_____.

5. My home address is

_____.

6. My Social Security Number is

_____.

7. Driver's license number and issuing state for any license issued in the past ten (10) years:

    No. _____ issued in the State of _____.

    No. _____ issued in the State of _____.

No. _____ issued in the State of _____.

8. I am _____ (male or female).

9. My race is

_____.

10. I request that my name be changed to

_____.

11. I want to change my name for the following reason:

_____
_____
_____
_____
_____
_____.

12. I do not have a SID (State Identification) or FBI (Federal Bureau of Investigation) number.

13. I have not been charged with a crime above the grade of Class C misdemeanor.

14. I have not had a final conviction of a felony.

15. I am not required to register as a sex offender, under Chapter 62 of the Texas Code of Criminal Procedure.

16. I have attached a legible and complete set of my fingerprints on a Department of Public Safety or Federal Bureau of Investigation fingerprint card to this Petition as Exhibit 'A' as required by Texas Family Code Section 45.102.

17. I respectfully ask that the Court issue an order changing my name to
_____ and ask that the Court grant me any other relief to which I am entitled, general or specific, legal or equitable.

RESPECTFULLY SUBMITTED:

_____
Signature

_____

_____
_____
_____

I, _____, Petitioner swear under oath that the facts stated in the above Original Petition for Change of Name of Adult are true and correct.

_____

_____
(This form should only be signed in the presence of a Notary Public.)

TO BE COMPLETED BY NOTARY:

SIGNED under oath before me on _____

_____
Notary Public, State of Texas

CAUSE NO._____

IN THE MATTER OF THE: §   IN THE DISTRICT COURT OF
                                         §
                                         §
                                         §
CHANGE OF NAME OF   §   _____ COUNTY, TEXAS
_____   §
                                         §
                                         §
                                         §
AN ADULT   §   JUDICIAL DISTRICT _____
                                         §
                                         §

ORDER GRANTING CHANGE OF NAME OF ADULT

On _____, this Court heard the Original Petition for Change of Name of Adult of
_____, Petitioner.

Petitioner appeared in person and announced ready.

The Court finds that it has jurisdiction of the case and of
_____, Petitioner.

[The Court Will Select One of the Following]

      [   ] Testimony was not recorded, and the Court agreed that it did not need to be recorded.

      [   ] Testimony was recorded by the official court reporter for the Court.

The Court finds the following information regarding the Petitioner:

1. Petitioner is: an adult.

2. Current full name:
_____.

3. Date of birth:
_____.

4. Place of birth:
_____.

5. Home address:
_____.

6. Social Security Number:

_____.

7. Driver's license number and issuing state for any license issued in the past ten (10) years:

No. _____ issued in the State of _____.

No. _____ issued in the State of _____.

No. _____ issued in the State of _____.

8. Petitioner is: _____ (male or female).

9. Petitioner's race is:

_____.

10. Petitioner does not have a SID (State Identification) or FBI (Federal Bureau of Investigation) number.

11. Petitioner has not been charged with a crime above the grade of Class C misdemeanor.

12. Petitioner has not had a final conviction of a felony.

13. Petitioner is not required to register as a sex offender under Chapter 62 of the Texas Code of Criminal Procedure.

14. Petitioner attached a legible and complete set of Petitioner's fingerprints on a Department of Public Safety or Federal Bureau of Investigation fingerprint card to the Petition.

15. Petitioner's change of name is in the interest or to the benefit of Petitioner and is in the interest of the public.

IT IS, THEREFORE, ORDERED that Petitioner's name is changed from

_____ to _____.

IT IS FURTHER ORDERED that all relief requested in this case not expressly granted is denied.

SIGNED on _____ by PRESIDING JUDGE

_____

JUDGE PRESIDING

CIVIL CASE INFORMATION SHEET

Cause Number (For Clerk Use Only): _____

Court (For Clerk Use Only):

_____

Styled: In the Matter of the Change of Name of _____, an
Adult

A civil case information sheet must be completed and submitted when an original petition or application is filed to initiate a new civil, family law, probate, or mental health case or when a post-judgment petition for modification or motion for enforcement is filed in a family law case. The information should be the best available at the time of filing. This sheet, approved by the Texas Judicial Council, is intended to collect information that will be used for statistical purposes only. It neither replaces nor supplements the filings or service of pleading or other documents as required by law or rule. The sheet does not constitute a discovery request, response, or supplementation, and it is not admissible at trial.

1. Contact information for person completing case information sheet:

Name:

_____

Address:

_____

_____

E-mail:

_____

Telephone:

_____

Fax:

_____

State Bar No:
N/A

Signature:

_____

Names of parties in case:

Plaintiff(s)/Petitioner(s):

_____

Defendant(s)/Respondent(s):
N/A

Person or entity completing sheet is:
[ ]   Attorney for Plaintiff/Petitioner
[X]   Pro Se Plaintiff/Petitioner
[ ]   Title IV-D Agency
[ ]   Other: _____

2. Indicate case type, or identify the most important issue in the case:

Family Law

Other Family Law
[ ]   Enforce Foreign Judgment
[ ]   Habeas Corpus
[X]   Name Change
[ ]   Protective Order

[ ]   Removal of Disabilities of Minority

[ ]   Other: _____

Need Legal Advice from a Virtual Attorney?

There is a new breed of lawyer that is committed to providing fixed fee limited legal services over the Internet. Often called "virtual lawyers" these practitioners offer legal advice for a fixed fee online and many offer name change legal forms bundled with legal advice also for a fixed fee.

- Lawyers who offer their legal services online offer these benefits:
- Lower overhead means lower fees;
- Fast Service;
- Accessible 24 x 7;
- Convenience – you don't have to give up hours during your work day to meet with a lawyer face to face in a downtown office building.

Check out SmartLegalForm's nationwide Directory of Virtual Law Firms at http://www.directlawconnect.com.

Do You Want Your Documents Reviewed by a Legal Document Assistant?

SmartLegalForms employs a team of legal document assistants, also known as Legal Technicians, who will provide a review of your forms to make sure that you have answered every question and that spelling and other information is internally consistent. We cannot give you legal advice. This service is available at the Web site: http://www.texasnamechangelaw.com . When you take advantage of this service we give you a credit for the price you paid for this book towards the Legal Document Preparation Service Fee.

For additional information, just email: support@smartlegalforms.com indicating the date of purchase of this book in the subject line of your email. You can also call our Help Line at: 1-800-481-1025

www.ingramcontent.com/pod-product-compliance
Lightning Source LLC
Chambersburg PA
CBHW040341220326
41518CB00044B/180